T0414096

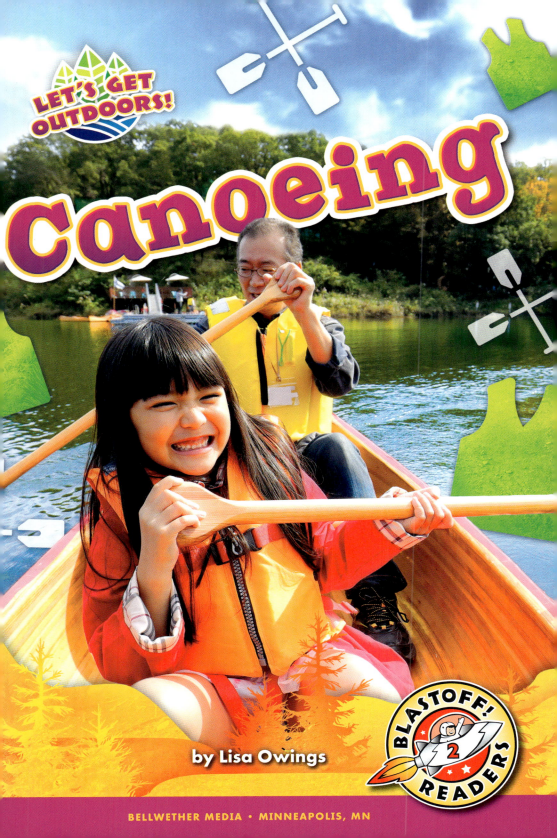

LET'S GET OUTDOORS!

Canoeing

by Lisa Owings

BLASTOFF! 2 READERS

BELLWETHER MEDIA • MINNEAPOLIS, MN

Blastoff! Readers are carefully developed by literacy experts to build reading stamina and move students toward fluency by combining standards-based content with developmentally appropriate text.

Level 1 provides the most support through repetition of high-frequency words, light text, predictable sentence patterns, and strong visual support.

Level 2 offers early readers a bit more challenge through varied sentences, increased text load, and text-supportive special features.

Level 3 advances early-fluent readers toward fluency through increased text load, less reliance on photos, advancing concepts, longer sentences, and more complex special features.

LEVELS

★ **Blastoff! Universe**

Reading Level

Grade **K**

Grades **1–3**

Grade **4**

This edition first published in 2023 by Bellwether Media, Inc.

No part of this publication may be reproduced in whole or in part without written permission of the publisher. For information regarding permission, write to Bellwether Media, Inc., Attention: Permissions Department, 6012 Blue Circle Drive, Minnetonka, MN 55343.

Library of Congress Cataloging-in-Publication Data

LC record for Canoeing available at: https://lccn.loc.gov/2022038747

Text copyright © 2023 by Bellwether Media, Inc. BLASTOFF! READERS and associated logos are trademarks and/or registered trademarks of Bellwether Media, Inc.

Editor: Rebecca Sabelko   Series Design: Andrea Schneider   Book Designer: Laura Sowers

Printed in the United States of America, North Mankato, MN.

LOS LOROS

por Genevieve Nilsen

TABLA DE CONTENIDO

tadpole
en español

PALABRAS A SABER

alas

árboles

garras

pico

plumas

vuelan

LOS LOROS

¡Veo un loro!

Él tiene un pico.

pico

Él come.

garra

Él tiene garras.

Los loros viven
en árboles.

pluma

Ellos tienen plumas.

Ellos tienen alas.

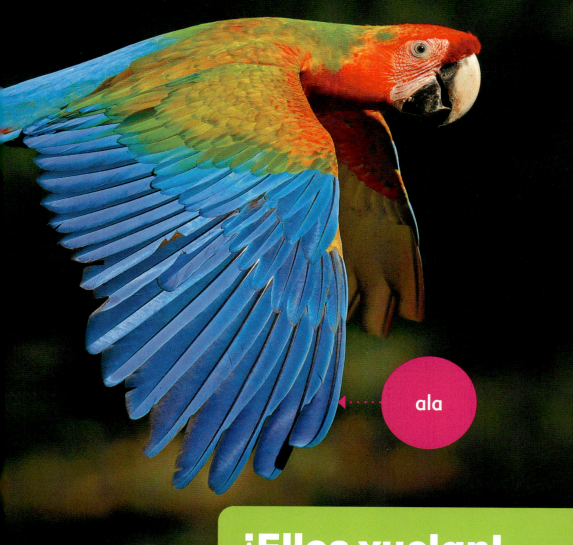

ala

¡Ellos vuelan!

13